Empowering Priesthood

A celebration of the ministerial priesthood
representing Christ to help form his body

Published by
Tufton Books
7 Tufton Street

Print Management by Shop4print

ISBN 085 191 0440

CONTENTS

PREFACE

'The glad tidings of Christianity are in what Jesus Christ did for men and in the abiding energy of that work'. So wrote Fr. Bull, one of the most energetic priests of the Community of the Resurrection, in the 1930's. His preaching drew Yorkshire people from up and down the Calder Valley to the Sunday afternoon mission services in the Quarry Theatre at Mirfield.

Empowering priesthood like Fr. Bull's seems scarce at the dawn of the Third Christian Millennium, as is priestly confidence in 'the abiding energy' of the work of Jesus Christ which is its basis. Yet Christ indeed retains the energy of his priesthood 'by the power of an indestructible life' (Hebrews 7:16). The ministerial priesthood which continues in the Church is called as ever to be instrument of that empowering. 'Far from diminishing his priesthood theirs is the continuation of its glory' (1).

A crisis of confidence in the priesthood affects the vitality of the Church and her mission, which is the overflow of her life. What is needed is 'not only…pragmatic models of (the priesthood's) functioning but horizons and visions of its meaning and its truth' (2)

The purpose of this book is to reopen some of these horizons by drawing afresh on the great Christian tradition. It echoes the sentiment of 2 Timothy 1:6-7 in its appeal for renewed confidence: 'Hence I remind you to rekindle the gift of God that is with you through the laying on of hands, for God did not give us as spirit of timidity but a spirit of power and love and self-control'.

I write in the year of my silver jubilee as a priest. Over twenty five years I have served four parishes, helped in the theological training of priests and most recently served as a mission officer, which has opened my eyes to the frustrations felt by many clergy today.

In recent years priests have presided over a severe decline in Church membership affecting their morale. At the same time serious questions have been raised about the ministerial priesthood itself. There is an attitude emerging that so emphasises lay ministry as to reduce priesthood to little more than a managerial function. A multitude of schemes have arisen to promote Church growth with very few having anything creative to say about the role of the ministerial priesthood in itself.

'The most urgent need in the Church today' we hear said 'is for leadership'. The implication is that the Church needs leaders more than she needs priests. 'The word leader is now being used as a substitute for... priest...there is a danger of a gap opening between a popular understanding of what ordination is about ('leadership') and the Church's understanding of that ministry captured in its liturgy and especially in the ordinals, which do not use the word' (3).

The gap spoken of can be closed by one of two means. Either the ordinal can be changed and the idea of ministerial priesthood rejected or the Church recovers the priestly understanding of ordination as an instrument of empowering.

Just over a century ago a commentator on a Church crisis of his day penned words that resonate with our own situation: 'I suppose that the deepest cleavage at the present moment in the Church of England is that between those who hold and those who deny the priestly character of the Ministry' (4)

This book is unashamedly *for* the 'priestly character of the Ministry' as a gift to the universal Church guaranteeing its Godward focus and the centrality of Christ. The author attempts a celebration of the ministerial priesthood as traditionally received, representing Christ to help form his body, serving union with God and the ultimate unity of the human race. Those who hold reservations about the 'priestly character of the Ministry' are invited into dialogue with this restatement of traditional faith, which has an eye to the better serving of the vitality and mission of the Church.

In addressing the 'triple office' of Christ as priest, prophet and shepherd king I go back to three basics of human existence - love, truth and power. The balancing of these three makes or breaks the world. Where is the desire to love without the power to do so? How can power be creative without love? Can the power to love serve anyone without the guidance of truth? In Christianity we see a balancing of love, truth and power and we see it in Jesus. His triple office reflects this balance, a balance to be exercised by those who particularly represent his priesthood for the building up of his body in worship, fellowship, mission and service.

After the initial explorations of Chapters 1 and 2 this book attends in Chapters 3-5 to the representation of Christ's triple office as priest, prophet and shepherd. The remaining chapters are concerned with the gift of discernment and how priests work for the transformation of lives. The last Chapter returns to the centrality of Christ as the One who has power to draw people to himself when he is lifted up in the Church.

The author would like to acknowledge the assistance of the Diocese of London, Sion College, the United Society for the Propagation of the Gospel and the Guyana Diocesan Association for their assistance towards the leave that facilitated this study. In particular he would like to thank the Bishop of Guyana and the parishes of St. Sidwell and the Transfiguration with St. Aloysius Chapel for their hospitality.

A special thankyou is due to Chris Davies, Kate Tattersall, Fr. Tim Bugby and the people of St. Augustine, Highgate for their assistance in the preparation of the book cover. Last but not least the author is grateful to his family for bearing with his absence on Study Leave and to his mother-in-law, Doris Scott, for proof reading this text.

John Twisleton

Haywards Heath

Feast of St. Thomas the Apostle
3rd July 2002

CHAPTER 1

BELIEVING IN THE PRIESTHOOD

Forget the priesthood and the Church becomes an institution for man's conversion instead of a spiritual temple for God's worship. H.S.Box

'God created the priest; and the devil, in revenge, created the clergy.' It can be true. There is a large Church I know. Someone related to me impressions of the priests they had seen at work in it over many years. 'I see them going one of two ways', he said. 'Either they grow grand and self-important like the building or they grow servant hearts in gratitude for the privilege of their appointment.'

T.S.Eliot observed that most of the trouble in the world is caused by people wanting to be important and the Church has no exemption from such trouble. So often the progress of the kingdom of God on earth is undermined by those who would build their own kingdom.

Believing in the ministerial priesthood is very different to believing in oneself as a priest. It is rather the opposite. We are 'pygmies in giant's armour' in Austin Farrer's memorable phrase. For the good of the Church we vest to represent Christ but, as Farrer also said, 'there is no more laughable sight than a priest vesting for the Eucharist.' Those who believe Christ becomes present in unique fashion through the prayer of the Eucharist should most fully recognise that such a miracle is no miracle personal to the priest but to his office and to the faithfulness of God in Christ.

'God created the priest...the devil...the clergy.' Clericalism is a pejorative term and concerns the misuse of a God-given office. Of all negative images of the priest that of one who suppresses spiritual vitality is the most infamous. All 'fizz' in the Church is stifled, in one famous image, by the 'cork in the bottle' - the parish priest! Let him out and the Spirit will flow in his Church, they say. Leave him be and you will never get God's people going forwards in mission.

It is a parody, of course. Yet there are indeed those among the clergy who 'hold the form of religion but deny the power of it' (1 Timothy 3:5). The call for renewed spiritual leadership in the Church can be threatening to many priests. Consequently some of those impatient for growth see the institutional priesthood as an obstacle to be removed.

H.S.Box once imagined the consequences of abandoning the ministerial priesthood. 'Forget the priesthood and the Church becomes an institution for man's conversion instead of a spiritual temple for God's worship; the prophet preaching to man supersedes the priest ministering to God; sacrifice becomes an obsolete idea, and religion is regarded rather as a satisfaction of man's need than as a yielding to God's claim' (5).

In its essence the priesthood secures the Church to the primacy of worship and the claim of God upon her.

1

THE PRIESTHOOD OF CHRIST

In Christianity there is one priest. Jesus Christ the Son of God has come into the world to bind humankind and all that is to himself and to make a perfect offering to God. The letter to the Hebrews speaks of his priesthood and eternal sacrifice as well as of the 'sacrifice of praise' of Christians. The first letter of Peter portrays the baptised as living stones in a living temple from which the sacrifice of praise rises to God. The New Testament speaks repeatedly of the privilege of believers becoming living instruments of God in Christ. They are caught up in the exercise of Christ's priesthood, which brings humanity to God and God to humanity. The book of Revelation addresses praise to Jesus Christ 'who loves us and has freed us from our sins by His blood and made us a kingdom, priests to His God and Father' (Revelation 1:5-6).

Elsewhere in the New Testament we read of the calling out of an apostolic ministry to serve this Godward calling of the whole priestly people of God. Saint Paul particularly mentions his 'priestly service of the Gospel of God' (Romans 15:16). He also exercises Church discipline 'in the person of Christ' (2 Corinthians 2:10). Although the New Testament references to the Church's leaders as priestly are in fact few, the understanding of ordained ministry that emerges from the apostolic era is priestly and linked to the Eucharist.

Austin Farrer draws a famous analogy between the emergence of episcopacy and ministerial priesthood as providential gifts to the Church and the emergence of the Canon of Scripture itself. 'The apostolic testimony was a divine gift; it settled into the scriptures of the New Covenant and we have canonised the scriptures. The apostolic ministry was likewise a divine gift; it settled into the episcopate and we have canonised the office' (6).

A SUBORDINATE LAITY?

In Christian tradition the one priesthood of Jesus Christ is held to operate in his Church drawing all the baptised into his worship of the Father and his quest for the outsider. The so-called 'ministerial priesthood' of bishops and priests provides 'a kind of sectional, emphasised witness to that which is true of the whole' (7).

In an ordination address Pope John Paul II underlines the missionary and empowering calling of priests: 'This gift of the priesthood, always remember, is a miracle that was realised in you but not for you. It was realised for the Church, which is equivalent to saying, for the world that must be saved. The sacred dimension of the priesthood is completely ordained to the apostolic dimension, namely, to mission, to the pastoral ministry. "As the Father has sent me, even so I send you" (John 20:21)' (8).

This traditional view of the priest as someone sent by Christ 'to make his priesthood present and effective to his people' (9) is criticised by Robin Greenwood as instituting 'permanent subordination' of the laity. He argues for the rejection of the personal representation of Christ in favour of a model he presents based on the Trinity, emphasising collaboration of clergy and laity. He insists that 'there is no difference between clergy and laity in the quality of their Christian authority' (10).

The misuse of the office of priest by its bearers contributed to the Reformation in the sixteenth century when Christians divided over the nature of the ordained ministry. The misuse of the theological distinction between clergy and laity is however no grounds for its dismissal. Christian tradition has never claimed that clergy are given more of the Holy Spirit than laity. St. Augustine, for example, was emphatic in speaking to his people: 'with you, I am a Christian; for you, I am a Bishop'. The special anointing in the Holy Spirit for the work of a bishop or priest has, at least officially, been seen as a gift through them to the whole Church and not as a personal possession. 'The whole body is priestly, but unless there are organs who express in a definite concrete form that priestly aspect of life which is directed to God, the whole body tends to lose its priestly attitude' (7)

THE PRIEST'S REPRESENTATIVE ROLE

In his book 'A Priesthood in Tune' Thomas Lane defends the special representative role of priests as essential to the centring of the Church upon Christ. Because of the brokenness and disorder intrinsic to the human condition all ministry must be related to Christ the Redeemer, who is Prophet, Priest and King. Christ gives to his Church the same mission of prophecy, priesthood and shepherding. This mission is strengthened and held to Christ by a ministerial priesthood having 'a particular sacramental relationship with Christ as High Priest' (ARCIC Elucidations, No 12). Whilst the ordained act uniquely 'in the person of Christ', all the baptised are called to so act on his behalf. 'The candles of both are lit from the one Paschal Candle, and, in turn, they help to light each other' (11).

If the Church exists primarily for worship, it is worship through, with and in Jesus Christ who 'ever intercedes' (Hebrews 7:25). The role of the clergy in representing Christ in the liturgy is seen by Lane as guaranteeing his centrality, not their own. In a musical analogy parallel to that of the candle he writes of the voices of priest, people and the interceding Christ as together shaping a 'sonata' of praise that glorifies God.

The distinction between the ministerial priesthood and that of the baptised is upheld in the Anglican - Roman Catholic agreement on Ministry and Ordination paragraph 13. Ordained ministry, ARCIC says, is 'not an extension of the common Christian priesthood but belongs to another realm of the gifts of the Spirit' (12). The necessity of this distinction links also to the important ministry of handing on apostolic teaching over which bishops and priests are seen to preside in the name of Christ. In a fast changing world this challenging ministry is a most necessary 'charism' noted in the traditional understanding of ordination. Once again it is the necessity to adhere to Christ and his teaching that is seen to lie behind the setting apart of some Christians through ordination to act for him as teacher.

SACRED MINISTRY

In his volume 'Elucidations' the late Hans Urs Von Balthasar writes of 'The Priest I Want'. There are some telling word pictures of the clergy. First the self-important priest - 'stupid, crafty, busy and imposing. He wants to be heard, he rushes to get on the media. He lies like mildew on the fields of the Church today.' Then there is the self-forgetful priest - 'become so unimportant to himself that for him only God still counts. Who he himself is, is no longer of any concern to him' (13). To Balthasar, ministerial priesthood is supremely 'sacred ministry' without presumption, modelled on the self-surrender of Jesus and the self-giving of St. Paul.

Many twentieth century theologians worked to recover emphasis upon the humanity of Christ and to challenge thinking in the Church that appeared to deny it. A parallel shift of emphasis can be discerned in thinking about the ordained ministry over the same period, so that the very term 'sacred ministry' sounds uncomfortable to the ears of many. Michael Ramsey's famous comment on the Jesus of John Robinson's 'Honest to God' needs to be translated to our thinking about our priests: 'The Man for Others is also the Man for God.'

Furthermore much questioning of the doctrines of the atonement has led many preachers to avoid the traditional metaphors of Christ's redemption such as 'sacrifice', 'substitution' and 'ransom' so that some correction is necessary. In his book 'A Spiritual Theology of the Priesthood' Dermot Power, disciple of Balthasar, defends the traditional metaphors still abounding in Church hymns. He sees them as providing the most effective witness to the 'recklessness of divine love'. If God seeks 'shepherds after his own heart' (Jeremiah 3:15) he will find them only as the Church reflects more fully upon the 'divine recklessness and magnanimity' shown in what Jesus has done for us. Truly 'sacred ministry' will emerge as the ministerial priesthood is affirmed as bearing indeed a special 'imaging' of Jesus to the Church. The grandeur and objectivity of such ministry needs receiving but alongside 'interiority', obedient love as the fount of a missionary priesthood (2).

Whereas Robin Greenwood distrusts what he calls the 'linear' view of priesthood commissioned by Christ in apostolic succession in favour of a 'relational' Trinitarian model, Power and others sense that it is this very link with Christ that guarantees the missionary element so vital to the Church. Greenwood's analysis is correct, in that, as he puts it, the Church must progress 'from… a haphazard assembling of passive individuals led by clergy, to one of corporate missionary agency in which the ministries of the whole Church and the ordained are bound to each other' (10). Yet, in rejecting the 'linear' sense of the priest as 'sent' in Christ's name and person to help form Christians, Greenwood undermines the mission impetus that a truly 'sacred ministry' might offer 'as servants (of the Church) for Jesus sake' (2 Corinthians 4:5b).

REFERENCES

1. J.M.Perrin *The Minister of Christ* 1964
2. Dermot Power *A Spiritual Theology of the Priesthood* 1998
3. Steven Croft *Ministry in Three Dimensions* 1999
4. W. Sanday *The Conception of Priesthood in the Early Church* 1898
5. H.S.Box (Editor) *Priesthood* quoted in Raymond Raynes *Called by God* 1959
6. A.M.Farrer quoted in G. Guiver et al *The Fire and the Clay* 1993
7. Raymond Raynes *Called by God* 1959
8. Pope John Paul II *A Priest for Ever* 1981
9. General Synod Report *Priesthood of the Ordained Ministry* 1986
10. Robin Greenwood *Transforming Priesthood* 1994
11. Thomas Lane *A Priesthood in Tune* 1993
12. Anglican-Roman Catholic Commission (ARCIC) *Ministry and Ordination* 1973
13. Hans Urs von Balthasar *Elucidations* 1971

CHAPTER 2
CONSECRATING PEOPLE

For their sake I consecrate myself, that they may also be consecrated in truth John 17:19
RSV

In Britain today many who recognise the importance of the spiritual dimension of life have come to seek engagement with eastern religions. Somehow Buddhism has come across to them as being more serious about truth and practical about spirituality than the Church.

This drift away from the Church does say something about her godliness. Her own prophets continually warn the Established Church that 'the Church of England needs to be converted so that it may become the Church of God in England' (1).

It could be said that the Church needs holiness even more than leadership in this age. However much we import management insight, we will end up managing decline unless there is a fresh kindling of holiness and consecration.

Spiritual revival is a process like the spreading of fire, starting from a minority, transforming the whole mass of God's people. The way to revival is not something to be engineered. It is a work of God made possible through the surrender of hearts.

RAISING MEN FROM THE EARTH

A priest is called in Michael Ramsey's phrase 'to be on the Godward side of human situations'. The former Archbishop of Canterbury goes on to quote Hooker: 'the power of the Ministry of God …raiseth men from the earth, and bringeth God himself down from heaven'. This raising is intrinsic to both the office and the spirituality of the priest. In Ramsey's memorable summary, priesthood is about 'being with God with the people on your heart' (2).

As 'messenger' the priest is one sent 'to teach and to admonish, to feed and to provide for the Lord's family'. Priests carry with them this ordination charge about forming the Christian community. 'Serve them with joy, build them up in faith, and do all in your power to bring them to loving obedience to Christ' (3).

The call to obedience is linked to the idea of consecration. Obedience in Christianity is not so much the forgoing of life but the redirecting of one's energies to God's praise and service. It is perfectly imaged in the incarnate life of Jesus. There we do not see a shunning of the world but life lived 'to the full' (John 10:10b). In his 'high priestly prayer' later in St. John's Gospel Jesus speaks directly of this consecration: 'As you have sent me into the world, so I have sent them into the world. And for their sakes I sanctify myself, that they also may be sanctified in truth.' (John 17:18-19).

One of the great heroes of the 20th Century Church of England was Frank Weston (1871-1924). Frank worked as the first Bishop of Zanzibar. He was to see his

Cathedral built upon the site of the former slave market on that island. His ministry centred upon Jesus in the Eucharist, in the poor and in the consecrated hearts of all his faithful people. He writes of the grace that flows through the consecration of day to day circumstances:

'The whole life of prayer for us who have to live in the world, the whole meaning of prayer, primarily, is the consecration of our circumstances, the redemption of an atmosphere in which the will of God can be manifested and in which Jesus can work' (4)

Frank Weston's life was fired by such consecration of his life day by day in the Eucharist. It is especially in the Eucharist that Christians experience the repeated call to consecration.

An empowering priesthood is one mindful of how the ordained priest acts in a special way to call the Christian community beyond itself to consecration in God, and does this supremely at the Eucharist. 'The function of the President is to represent the initiating and transcendent self-giving of Christ who himself bestows on the community what it cannot by its own spiritual energies achieve...Eucharist is not a self-actualising process; it is a gift and it is a coming...it lifts people out of themselves into a communion that is the whole Church...(the community) becoming less its own centre and finding its centre in Christ, and through him, with him and in him the abyss of Triune love for the world' (5).

ONE WHO CONFRONTS WITH THE GOSPEL

Consecration of life is the work of the Holy Spirit. By his power Jesus is experienced in the Church as personal Saviour. Christians are called to do business with God as individuals. 'Is there a specialist for God's relationship to me? One who makes Christ immediate? So that, given my natural disposition to shrink the demands of God, I can be confronted with the Gospel and held to it?'(6). So muses Balthasar, and he goes on to affirm 'on the basis of both his commission and of his experience (the priest) can embody both the relentlessness and the love which are to be found in God's will in such a way that one can no longer and will no longer run away'.

This is the ideal, 'the Priest I want' in Balthasar's phrase, 'one who confronts with the Gospel'. It is as if a particular ministry is called for by the very particularity of Christianity, which has a particular Saviour who is particularly represented to his Church through the priesthood.

The sacrament of absolution gives a striking illustration of how the setting apart of one to act for Christ enables a rite of welcome for sinners. God's forgiveness is granted immediately to the one who is penitent but it is their sensing and laying hold of this that is transformative. In the Evangelical tradition, the scripture promises are seen as almost tangible assurance of forgiveness. The acted-out rite of reconciliation gives another assurance. It provides a sacrament, a tangible means of welcoming forgiveness, in which the priest uses the authority given at ordination to draw individuals through words of forgiveness into a deeper consecration of life. 'Whose sins thou dost forgive, they are forgiven'.

CALL TO RENEWAL

'The God who brings light out of darkness', writes St. Paul, 'also shines in our hearts to give the light of the knowledge of the glory of God in the face of Jesus Christ' (2 Corinthians 4:6).

There is something ever new about Jesus Christ. Wherever he is welcomed 'light' and 'glory' shine. Just over a century after the resurrection St. Irenaeus wrote of Jesus Christ that he had 'brought all newness by bringing his own person'. Into all that is tired and faded in human life Jesus brings a perpetual gift of renewal.

The so-called 'spiritual gifts' listed in scripture are gifts of renewal from the risen Christ. Through the charismatic movement the more extraordinary gifts of healing, miracles, tongues etc. (1 Corinthians 12:4-11) are being recovered. Such gifts need to be welcomed alongside the institutional gifts: 'apostles, prophets, pastors and teachers' (Ephesians 4:11). The ministerial priesthood has been recognised in the Christian tradition as also a gift of the Spirit to be welcomed as a continual source of renewal alongside the more charismatic gifts. 'Both Church and ministry are gifts of the divine Lord Jesus' (Michael Ramsey).

Empowering priesthood recognises that 'hierarchical' and 'charismatic' gifting are both given by God to work in harmony. The extraordinary gifts of the Spirit such as healing and prophecy are most effective when guided by those who hold pastoral oversight. Conversely as pastoral office bearers cooperate with those gifted in prayer and prophecy they too work as instruments of God's great purpose of 'building up the body of Christ, until we all attain to the unity of the faith and of the knowledge of the Son of God, to mature manhood, to the measure of the stature of the fullness of Christ' (Ephesians 4).

STEWARDS NOT PROPRIETORS

An empowering priesthood is one that sees itself as 'steward of the mysteries of God' (1 Corinthians 4:1). A steward is not a proprietor. Always there is tension in the Church between true stewardship and the proprietorial spirit. All movements of renewal remind the Church that she is a gift from God and gifted by God. She is not meant to belong to anyone under God. It is a message that challenges the ministerial priesthood to go with the flow of the Holy Spirit rather than to play safe as 'proprietors'.

Only too easily priests can misuse their authority to quench the Holy Spirit. This can come about especially in their treatment of spiritually gifted laity who so often appear as a challenge to their authority rather than as a resource, a gifting from God to build up his Church. Whilst such people need challenging at times, they also need

8

to be encouraged. Unless there is a recognition that spiritual leadership in the Church is not just in the hands of the clergy, the potential for growth is severely restricted.

An empowering priesthood assists the contribution of every member of the Church to her vitality and mission. It challenges proprietorial attitudes that deny this principle of stewardship. Sometimes the proprietorial spirit can appear as a form of partisanship. This is a particular challenge to priests who are bound to challenge party spirit since 'the partisan can soon become a person who loves his own apprehension of truth more than Christ, and himself (sic) more than either' (2).

THE PRIMACY OF THE MYSTICAL

Empowering priesthood calls forth a consecrated people, one that has wholeness in Christ yet with all diversity. Good practice in parishes seeks worship that is accessible whilst retaining powerful witness to the awe and mystery of God which calls forth consecration. 'Great indeed is the mystery of our religion' (1 Timothy 3:16) yet people who cross the Church's threshold today are not always brought to their knees. They sometimes seem more awed by eastern religion.

A priest was asked why he used incense in Church and answered 'because you cannot buy it in Marks and Spencer'. He sensed that the sure, unselfconscious majesty of Sunday worship in the great tradition of the Church can evoke an awe before the mystery of God which no self-conscious construct of ten minute 'sound-bites' can rival. Inevitably for the Church to be experienced more as the Church of *God*, it needs preachers, teachers and witnesses who can evoke more fully the awe and mystery of God's being, love and holiness.

An empowering priesthood seeks a true renewal in the Holy Spirit of every aspect of Church life including the exercise of the ministerial priesthood itself. A powerful description of the difference such renewal makes was expressed by an Orthodox bishop in a keynote address to the World Council of Churches.

> 'Without the Holy Spirit: God is far away,
> Christ stays in the past,
> he Gospel is a dead letter,
> the Church is simply an organisation,
> authority is a matter of domination,
> mission a matter of propaganda,
> the liturgy no more than an evocation,
> Christian living a slave morality

> 'But in the Holy Spirit:
> the cosmos is resurrected and groans
> with the birth-pangs of the Kingdom,

9

the risen Christ is there,
the Gospel is the power of life,
the Church shows forth the life of the Trinity,
authority is a liberating service,
mission is a Pentecost,
the liturgy is both memorial and anticipation,
human action is deified' (7).

Fresh empowerment of the Church of God comes from a recapturing of vision only God can provide by his Spirit. It cannot be forced by human demand or manipulation, it comes by grace.

Bishop Ignatios warned the World Council of Churches that Christianity without grace becomes a 'slave morality'. It is the frequent temptation of the priest as preacher and teacher to moralise and so to 'enslave'. Basic Christianity by contrast places the demands of morality second to the revelation of grace and mercy given by the Spirit in Jesus Christ. What distinguishes Christianity is something that goes beyond morality as such - something utterly transcendent.

To welcome the Christian revelation is to welcome the grace of the Holy Spirit, to see and recognise God in Christ as one more concerned to give us what we need than what we deserve.

An empowering priesthood shares this concern as one that reflects the very heart of God towards humanity. God seeks a consecrated people before he seeks the imposition of moral uniformity. Although priests have to hand on Christ's ethical teaching and not their own, this is therefore best done most often in parenthesis to teaching on the grace and mercy of God.

Much disillusionment seems to arise about the Church through her apparent moralising, although it is true that the mass media are very ready to distort things. Sometimes such moralising becomes a veiled form of worldliness in that it presents the distinctive feature of Christianity as superior moral achievement. As Henri Nouwen warns, 'when the moral life gets all the attention, we are in danger of forgetting the primacy of the mystical life, which is the life of the heart' (8).

Empowering priesthood calls God's people back to what is distinctive about Christianity and what makes them distinctive as those consecrated 'to proclaim the mighty acts of him who called (us) out of darkness into his marvellous light. Once (we) were not a people, but now (we) are a people; once (we) had not received mercy, but now (we) have received mercy' (1 Peter 2:9b-10).

REFERENCES

1. Michael Marshall *The Gospel Connection* 1990
2. Michael Ramsey *The Christian Priest Today* 1972
3. Ordination of Priests *The Alternative Service Book* 1980
4. Frank Weston *In His Will* 1914
5. Dermot Power *A Spiritual Theology of the Priesthood* 1998
6. Hans Urs Von Balthasar *Elucidations* 1971
7. Bishop Ignatios of Latakia *World Council of Churches Uppsala Report* 1968
8. Henri Nouwen *The Road to Daybreak* 1988

CHAPTER 3
BUILDING LOVE

In Jesus, priest, prophet and shepherd-king there is the perfect balancing of love, truth and power.

There is only one priest. Christianity is life in him. Jesus Christ brings perfect glory to God and full salvation to the world. As 'priest over the house of God', Jesus gives his household the Church, 'confidence to enter the sanctuary' in worship and, by his once for all offering 'full assurance of faith' and salvation (Hebrews 10:19-22).

In Jesus there is to be found the perfect combination of three qualities so dispersed in a broken world - love, truth and power. These qualities in the life of God are reflected in the triple office of Jesus shared with his Church - that of priest, prophet and king or shepherd.

'It is he whom we proclaim' writes St Paul, 'warning everyone and teaching everyone in all wisdom, so that we may present everyone mature in Christ. For this I toil and struggle with all the energy that he powerfully inspires within me.' (Colossians 1:28-9).

The same energy is to be at work in the 'apostles' of today seeking maturity in Christ in the Church. The Holy Spirit energises the clergy as they make themselves tools of his building up the life of Christ in love, truth and power.

> 'No one can say "Jesus is Lord" except by the *Holy Spirit*'
> (1 Corinthians 12:3b).
> 'God's *love* has been poured into our hearts through the Holy Spirit'
> (Rom 5:5b).
> 'When the Spirit of *truth* comes he will guide you into all the truth'
> (John 16:13a).
> 'You will receive *power* when the Holy Spirit has come upon you and
> you will be my witnesses' (Acts 1:8a).

Working under the authority of and in the person of Christ and empowered by his Spirit, the ministerial priesthood looks to the consecration and maturing of the Church in love, truth and powerful witness. The balancing of these qualities is expressed in the three titles of priest, prophet and shepherd king traditionally ascribed to Christ

In this Chapter and the two that follow attention will be given to how an empowering priesthood acts for Christ as priest, prophet and shepherd in building up the Church.

12

THIS IS MY BODY GIVEN FOR YOU

A friend who is a priest once confided in me that he had become more and more 'Calvinistic' in his view of human nature as his ministry had proceeded. Somehow he had lost his original optimism about the people he dealt with in the Church. He expected the negative. Despite that perception he was still a highly convivial priest who helped generate a convivial Christian community. Yet, in his heart he was somewhat broken by his experience over his years of priesthood. He had learned that as God treats us as better than we are so must we Christians endeavour to treat our fellows - the Lord being our helper.

There is something dismaying about a priest who holds contempt for his people. Lack of love in the Church is a major flaw and sign of her human inadequacy. Because her members are chosen for her and do not choose themselves or one another, finding the love to build an effective Christian community is an essential priority to be addressed by her leaders.

'Remember always with thanksgiving that the treasure now to be entrusted to you is Christ's own flock, bought through the shedding of his blood on the cross' (1).

Contemporary talk of love shows at times a shallowness that hardly measures up to the Christian use of that word, which honours the sacrificial gift of Jesus himself. 'I love you' so often means 'I love me and want you'. In Christ, 'I love you' means 'This is my body given for you'. The ministry of priests preserves those words which, read at every Eucharist, define and challenge the Christian community.

Empowering the Church is a matter of facing this challenge of love, which relates to both the truth and power which are also granted in Jesus. Any reading of the lives of the Saints quickly evidences that the love of God and neighbour has been a struggle all through Christianity. Conviction about the truth of Christ and the empowering of grace has always been necessary to help the Saints prevail in love.

CHALLENGING THE STRONG

Love is a gift to be given and to be welcomed in the Church. The self-sufficiency of contemporary humankind has so invaded her that there are many problems about both giving and receiving love. Yet only as love is built can a parish Church be 'of' rather than 'for' the people.

Priests have something of a task in helping the Christian community 'break in' some of her stronger members. There can be insensitivity about the more indomitable Christian. C.S.Lewis drew a picture of one such lady 'who spent her energies in the service of others'. He added, 'you could tell "the others" by their hunted look!' In such cases priests need courage to get alongside these stronger members and help their fuller consecration.

Sometimes the more confident and energetic members of a Church, like Lewis's lady, are incapable of receiving love themselves. Many priests even find the welcoming of love very difficult themselves. They have been so schooled in independence that the admission of a need for love is almost anathema.

The priest helps build love in the Church by challenging the strong to deeper sensitivity and vulnerability. The channelling of people's strengths to God's praise and service is as helpful to a loving Christian community as the misuse of those strengths is damaging. Priestly ministry is about helping people consecrate their strengths to God, which sometimes requires encouraging them first to 'let God love them'.

BUT FOR THE GRACE OF GOD...

Building love in the Church links to the growth in humility and a sense of people's need of grace. Only as people are confident enough to 'be themselves' does a community really form. 'All of us who are part of the community know our individual failings, yet while we are there we are lifted into something greater than any of us could achieve alone...Our places of worship are about turning strangers into friends...There is no greater source of peace - peace of the soul - than this, knowing that we are known, recognising that we are recognised. Then I understand how community is the human expression of Divine love. It is where I am valued simply for who I am, how I live and what I give to others. It is the place where they know my name' (2).

One of the great weaknesses of the clergy is failure to trust. Sometimes it is the experience of betrayal that stops the honesty basic to building up a community of trust. Bearing graciously with petty 'betrayals' is essential if a priest is to be Christ's instrument of building love. This is perhaps why someone wrote once that 'at the centre of every "living" parish there is a "dying" priest'.

Priesthood is a matter of connecting people one to another through connecting them with Christ. It is said that the place of greatest solidarity in the world is among those who see themselves in some sense as at the foot of the Cross of Christ. Though ordained priests represent Christ's merciful forgiveness through their office, where they are able to witness truthfully and without scandal to their own personal need for mercy, they definitely enhance the work of reconciliation among Christians.

'There but for the grace of God go I' said the Puritan watching the condemned man ascend the scaffold. A sense of mercy needs cultivating in the Church today so that she is seen as an oasis of mercy in a judgmental world. We are said to live in a culture of contempt where the mass media continually exposes human frailty and judges it without forgiveness. The miracle of Christianity is a God who is less concerned to give people what they deserve than to give them what they need. In building love in the Church priests and people are being prophetic, speaking of the truth of God which empowers and sets free.

14

SERVANT OF UNITY

'The vocation of all those who share in the priesthood of the one High Priest is to keep re-making in him the broken connections between earth and heaven where our High Priest is' writes Thomas Lane. 'The task of the person in ordained ministry is the continual making of connections between the word of God and the daily lives of people - between word, sacrament, and pastoral ministry. This must be done in continual partnership with Jesus Christ and with all those who exercise baptismal priesthood. The dream of God for the universe is a world in harmony, in tune. But the world fell out of harmony, in the mess we have come to call original sin. Into a world out of harmony and out of tune, the Son of God came saying 'See, God, I have come....to do your will, O God' (Hebrews 10:7). The letter to the Hebrews gives us his programme for the only true priesthood, the only true sacrifice, the only true at-one-ment, the only true in-tune-ment' (3).

In his high priestly prayer Jesus pleads for unity among his disciples 'so that the world may believe' (John 17:21). Over twenty centuries those in holy orders have served this unity basic to mission, albeit inadequately, so that by the visible unity of Christians there might be a sign or sacrament of unity for humankind.

'By all means have your special friends', wrote Monsignor Knox in his book 'On the Priestly Life'. 'Only be sure of one thing - be sure that everybody in the parish is your special friend as well!' (4). Building unity in the local Church can be very costly for priests. Yet, as Michael Ramsey addressed his priests, 'you will never be nearer to Christ than in caring for the one man, the one woman' (5).

The ministerial priesthood is itself, under the episcopacy, a sign guaranteeing the unity of the local Church with the universal Church. That sign of unity which is the priesthood has the potential to empower the local Church as it seeks to be 'one bread... one body' (1 Corinthians 10:17).

In a fragmented world, the unity of Christians in the grace of God continues as a challenge for 'the world to believe' in Christ, source of that unity. Yet for the Church to be empowered and invigorated by new members requires yet more costly efforts towards visible unity, both in congregations and between denominations.

The renewal of the Church in love is prior to her growth, for how can people accept the claims of Christ when they see lack of love in his Church?

REFERENCES

1.   Ordination of Priests *The Alternative Service Book* 1980
2.   Jonathan Sacks *Celebrating Life* 2000
3.   Thomas Lane *A Priesthood in Tune* 1993
4.   Ronald Knox *The Priestly Life* 1958
5.   Michael Ramsey *The Christian Priest Today* 1972

CHAPTER 4
CONVINCING AUTHORITY

Love and truth walk in your presence, Lord Psalm 89:14

In Chapter 3 attention was given to how an empowering priesthood serves the building up of the Church in love as it acts for Christ as priest. In this Chapter our focus moves on to the prophetic aspect of the ministerial priesthood. This aspect runs alongside the priestly and pastoral elements as sure as love, truth and power are to be found in Jesus.

Church growth surveys depict growing Churches as those that have attained a loving atmosphere open to the challenge of Christ's teaching and the empowering of his Spirit. Such Churches tend to have a leadership combining these qualities intrinsic to Jesus Christ in being friendly, principled and enthusiastic.

Mahatma Ghandi related his experience of the Christian Church in South Africa in the early part of the twentieth century. Hungry for a spirituality himself, he was disconcerted by the lack of interest in spiritual matters there. Apart from the lack of teaching ministry, the congregation he joined appeared to him more of a social club than a school of prayer. It was this perceived lack of seriousness about truth and spirituality that led him to move on from Christianity to recover his own native religion.

Where there is an emphasis upon a loving fellowship to the detriment of the teaching ministry the Church can appear shallow. Conversely where Gospel truth prevails over the human element, the Church can appear shrill and forbidding. The ultimate partnership of love and truth is affirmed several times in Scripture. In the Psalms, for example, we read this affirmation of their equal balance: 'love and truth walk in your presence, Lord' (Grail Psalter 89:14b).

As a community is formed in Christ there is a building in love, a consecration in truth and an empowering in the Holy Spirit. The ministerial priesthood plays an important role in achieving this balance in Christ.

Prophetic ministry relates the word of God to particular situations bringing challenge and urgency into people's considerations. This ministry of challenge so essential to the Church's mission is shared in measure by all the baptised as they help people interpret their personal situations in the light of Christ.

If all the baptised possess such spiritual authority, the ministerial priesthood, bears authority in a particular fashion. Bishops and priests bear authority as a gift to the Church as a whole. The triple office of Jesus - prophet, priest and king (shepherd) - is their particular witness as one section of the Church emphasising what is to become more and more true of the whole community.

'WE HAVE OUR ORDERS'

The good news of Christianity lies in what Jesus Christ did for the world and in the abiding energy of his work. The momentum of the Christian Faith has carried it through twenty centuries including periods of hostility or indifference.

Any community with a purpose is held on track by appropriate authority. The Christian Church claims to have been given authority by Jesus Christ to continue his saving mission of bringing all that is into fellowship with God. The scriptures and creeds, the orderly succession of bishops and Church Councils - all hold authority in the sense of holding Christianity to its divine purpose. The exercise of authority within the Church is ideally the instrument of the living Christ working through scripture, tradition and the reasoned consensus of Christians.

In facing up to Christian divisions over a remarkable century of convergence between the Churches, it has been widely recognised that authority and leadership within them is a sovereign gift of God to be welcomed as the servant of mission. 'Authority is exercised within the Church for the sake of those outside it, that the Gospel may be proclaimed "in power and in the Holy Spirit and with full conviction" (1 Thessalonians 1:5). This authority enables the whole Church to embody the Gospel and become the missionary and prophetic servant of the Lord' (1).

Church leaders are not seen to receive authority by their merits, and neither is the God-given authority within the Church totally invalidated by her failure to preserve Christian unity over the centuries. The ordained ministry is a gift to create this 'holy order' lifting the baptised up to God in worship and turning them outwards in love to humankind as a sacrament of salvation.

'Yet it is far from true that while the Church is our Lord's creation the ministry is only a device whereby the Church can be effective. Both Church and ministry are gifts of the divine Lord Jesus. He appointed twelve that they might be with him, and that he might send them forth. When he ascended on high he gave gifts to men. The apostle draws his commission and authority from Christ alone, and he uses an authority given to him when in Christ's name he ordains and commissions the presbyters. "Take thou authority for the office and work of a priest in the Church of God now committed unto thee by the imposition of these hands, and be thou a faithful dispenser of the word of God and of his holy sacraments....our consciousness is not of our own status, but of Christ whose commission we hold and of the people we serve in his name' (2).

The renewal of the priesthood requires a recovery of confidence in the teaching office of the priest. Priests need to be reminded that 'they have their orders' as a divine gift and calling. It is an unfashionable, military image but true to scripture and the Christian tradition. The ministerial priesthood shepherds, teaches and leads worship under clear authority handed down from the Founder of Christianity himself. At the same time 'to have convincing authority (they) must share the journeys of people, enter their fears, be touched by their disappointments, their questions, their failures and doubts' (3).

HUMILITY AND CONFIDENCE

'Convincing authority' is the very quality to be sought and re-established by the Church, starting with her leaders. Fr. Radcliffe points out how the sharing of life between priests and their people at a deep level helps them win respect for their office as well as their person. The numerical decline of the Western Church undoubtedly links to the rejection of authority in the sense of what is 'aloof' or 'institutional'. It links also though to a perception of the Church as a less than spiritual body. So many are seeking spirituality through eastern religions as if the grass were greener outside Christianity.

'Convincing authority' in a priest or bishop links to a costly involvement with God's people. More profoundly, it links to their own 'conviction' as persons called to be 'convincing' in what they teach. As with Moses and the burning bush, there needs to be a 'fire' that sets things going. Moses' mission was actually kindled by fire, by an encounter with God, cloaked in awe and mystery.

'Come no closer! Remove the sandals from your feet, for the place on which you are standing is holy ground' (Exodus 3:5).

Abraham, Joshua, Samson, Gideon, Samuel, David, Isaiah, Jeremiah, Mary, Paul...all find themselves convinced through encounters with God that are both personal and mysterious, moving them to worship.

Empowering priesthood cannot be 'fired' without the sort of humility bred from personal encounter with the mystery that is God, Father, Son and Holy Spirit. Only as the Church is brought to her knees before the splendour and holiness of God, only as she is compelled to 'take off her shoes', only as we, individually, encounter the mystery of Christ, will we be fired for the Kingdom of God.

Mainstream Christianity steers a middle course between exalting the authority of the ordained and exalting the need for their authentic experience and manifestation of Christ. The gift of order in the Church served by those in 'holy orders' is seen as something objective that prevails over the unworthiness of the office bearer. Priests who are not mindful that the Sacraments they celebrate are valid only despite their own unworthiness are guilty of presumption. Yet priests who put confidence in God to act through their priesthood irrespective of their own interior disposition are also presumptuous. Sacraments may be valid but ineffective because of the dispositions of the human participants.

St Francis de Sales speaks of two prime virtues in Christianity - *humility* and *confidence* in God. Where Christians are both 'struck by God', knowing their need of him, and have expectations of God to provide for them, the Holy Spirit can be made present to sanctify. By analogy priests need both confidence in their office and calling as priests, and humility before the mystery of God, to bear their office appropriately if they are to be effective for Christ. When the concept of the office of priests has been brought into question it has very often been through evident lack of humility in the exercise of that office.

Grace Kelly, an American film star, married Prince Rainier of Monaco. She was asked how she took to people coming and curtseying to her. 'It's my office and not my person that they honour' was her sharp reply. So it is over the honour given on occasion to priests, through whom people reverence a particular gift of his representation from Christ to the world.

There are certainly priests whose sense of the dignity of their office has become inseparable from a devilish self-importance. Yet there is a balancing constituency who are losing the energy and momentum Christ would lend to their office by latent cynicism about their calling. Loss of confidence and loss of humility are both serious failings in the ordained ministry, which undermine the spiritual vitality of the Church as a whole.

INSTITUTIONAL AND CHARISMATIC AUTHORITY

Scripture sees the Church as 'built upon the foundation of the apostles and prophets, with Christ Jesus himself as the cornerstone' (Ephesians 2:20). Apostolic and prophetic ministry are seen as inseparable there. In practice they have drifted apart. A distinction has grown up between the 'institutional' and 'charismatic' aspects of the Church, which can be seen as linked to the apostolic and foundational aspect and to the more dynamic and forward looking aspect expressed through the gift of prophecy.

One of the great challenges to the Church today is the reintegration of these aspects so that the charismatic essence may shine out through the dullness of her institutional structure.

Whereas the cultic role of priests leads the Church in her cycle of worship their prophetic role seeks to direct the community. There will always be creative tension between the 'cyclical' and 'directional' elements of the Church. They can be roughly identified with the complementary terms 'Catholic' and 'Evangelical'. 'Catholic' Churches which are strong on the cycle of worship often need to develop a greater sense of the pilgrim people of God 'following the Lord's leading'. Conversely the clear task-orientation of Churches focussed on outreach needs to be balanced by the recovery of worship as foundational. 'The Catholic Faith is this, we worship..' (Athanasian Creed).

Once again, we return to the inseparability of the priestly, prophetic and pastoral aspects of all ministry which in turn are faithful to the love, truth and empowering to be found in Jesus. In particular priests' preaching and teaching ministry balance their celebration of the Sacraments and their pastoral ministry following the same dynamic.

There is a saying in educational circles which runs: 'I hear, I forget. I see, I remember. I do, I understand'. It represents a formidable challenge to traditional Christian teaching e.g. the former memorising of the Catechism. At the same time, the visual and ritual aspects of the Faith illuminate and deepen its verbal proclamation. This can be particularly evident when preaching at the Eucharist summons self-offering to be acted out in the 'taking, blessing, breaking and sharing' rites. Similarly the liturgy of baptism is rich in symbolism yet needful of an appropriate message of challenge or personal testimony to bring out the element of empowering latent in the rites.

CHRISTIAN IDENTITY IN A POST-CHRISTIAN SOCIETY

As the minister who presides over baptism the priest has an eye to the holding together of liturgical, catechetical and pastoral considerations. The practice of infant baptism without the challenging of the parents to faith is a prophetic failure. At the same time too rigorous a baptism policy can undermine the priestly and pastoral aspects of Christ's care.

Perhaps the prophetic element is the more necessary in a post-Christian society. The whole consciousness of what it is to be a Christian is affected by the conduct of the rites of baptism. Here there is the clearest statement of Christian Faith and for it to be made with evident insincerity undermines the call to integrity. On the other hand, the Church's prophetic voice in baptism, the sacrament of conversion, will only be heard if it is in turn a loving voice. The time given to the pastoral care of the families involved is extremely important in gaining mutual understanding and respect for truth. The whole Church membership needs to be made aware through ongoing teaching of the dignity and responsibilities of baptism and so help interpret and defend it before the world.

In turn this raises the issue of Christianity in relation to modern culture, where there is flexibility and where there is inevitable conflict and even spiritual warfare. A counter-cultural emphasis is particularly to be found in the revised ordination service of the Church of England, preserved from a similar expression in the Book of Common Prayer. The Bishop addresses those to be ordained priest in these words: 'You are to be a messenger, watchman and steward of the Lord; you are to teach and to admonish, to feed and to provide for the Lord's family; to search for his children in the wilderness of this world's temptations and to guide them through its confusions, so that they may be saved through Christ for ever' (4).

COURAGE AND PRUDENCE

The teaching office of priests requires courage to proclaim the unfashionable as well as prudence to know how to do so most appropriately.

There is a Don Camillo story where the village priest has one of his many rows with the village Mayor. He goes into Church and kneels before the crucifix. 'Should I consult public opinion about this one, Lord?' he enquires. 'I shouldn't bother', the Lord replies from the Cross. 'Look what it did to me!'.

The Christian Faith is a school of courage and priests as 'public Christians' are inevitably teachers - and learners - in that school. To be courageous is to possess the God-given capacity to transform fear into something beautiful. The word 'courage' is linked to the heart - it means literally to take heart, to grow strong in heart. If the purpose of God is to form our hearts and give us courage, would that be possible if priestly ministry was without contention?

'This is the victory that conquers the world, our faith' writes St. John (1 John 5:4), who also reports these words of Jesus: 'Take courage, I have conquered the world' (John 16:33).

How can we be given such 'overcoming faith' without also being given things to overcome? How can we gain heart without at times having to brave disheartening circumstances?

Nevertheless courage always goes hand in hand with prudence. It is prudent to go gently in pastoral situations linked to the Church's teaching on sexual ethics. Such prudence needs to go hand in hand though with the courage to include such teaching within the overall scheme of catechesis. 'We have our orders'. There is a responsibility to hand on what we have received from the universal Church before our own private judgement. It cannot be handed on ungraciously but it must somehow be handed on. As someone expressed it in terms of the teaching of the sixth commandment, the gracious emphasis is '*Thou* shalt not commit adultery' 'rather than 'Thou shalt *not* commit adultery'. It is our sense of worth given by God that needs prime emphasis.

The wise priest brings in the hard teachings in parenthesis to a focus upon the grace of God and the dignity of the human person in his image. 'The body of Christ is galvanised not by knowledge alone nor teaching, nor conviction, but the presence of one who expands the horizons of what it is to be a person' (5).

REFERENCES

1. Anglican-Roman Catholic Commission (ARCIC)
    The Gift of Authority 1999
2. Michael Ramsey *The Christian Priest Today* 1972
3. Timothy Radcliffe *Sing a New Song* 1999
4. Ordination of Priests *The Alternative Service Book* 1980
5. G. Guiver et al *The Fire and the Clay* 1993

CHAPTER 5
EMPOWERING PRIESTHOOD

Empowerment is the business of the Church because it has always the energy of Jesus Christ

An empowering priesthood acts for Christ as priest, prophet and shepherd. In this Chapter attention is given to the third 'shepherding' or 'pastoral' ministry every priest holds in the name of Christ.

Good priests reduce unemployment in the Church. They see their task under Christ not just in terms of caring for their congregations but also in helping their congregations employ more of their caring gifts. 'The task of the ordained ministry is not simply to minister to the congregation but to create and direct a ministering congregation through the detection, development and deployment of God-given resources' (1).

RELEASING GIFTS

Many parishes are finding a use for the Lady Chapel on a Sunday morning. After the Parish Eucharist lay people with listening gifts stand by there to offer prayer for specific needs after the service. In this way personal matters that come to the surface through the experience of worship can be dealt with by a specific commending to God. Such prayer ministry frees their priest for the ministry of welcoming newcomers and dealing with the many practical matters that surface on a Sunday morning. This is a development reported as occurring throughout the Church of England in the recently published report on the healing ministry (2).

Among a multitude of observations about healing ministry the Report has one observation with a potential now being more realised than ever in pastoral ministry. 'There is nothing to prevent any Christian praying for a sick person on an appropriate occasion'.

At the same time the encouragement of such ministry of prayer is accompanied by new guidelines which honour the priest's and the bishop's oversight. 'No one should act in isolation; all should be trained as part of being 'under authority''. Priests are to foster the empowering of Church members in this realm whilst focussing the Gospel imperative 'to heal the sick' in their own sacramental ministries of confession and anointing. A balance is to be struck between too narrow a sacramental approach, downplaying the role of the laity, and too disordered a scheme, where pastoral damage can occur through misplaced enthusiasm.

The realm of the healing ministry is just one example of where an empowering priesthood is being instrumental in 'building up the body of Christ' (Ephesians 4:12b). This upbuilding is a process in which priests use their authority in Christ's name to empower the ministry of the baptised.

If priests are 'celebrants' of the Eucharist, that privilege brings with it the responsibility of generating a community of prayerful celebration. If they are preachers and prophets, it is to invigorate a witnessing community. Their pastoral role, as in ministry to the sick, is likewise one that releases pastoral gifts of service to be directed towards the work of God.

Surveys have demonstrated that a Church led by one priest can rarely grow beyond 150 members unless the Church appoints lay leaders and forms cell groups. In such groups people can know one another and grow together as Christians in faith, love and numbers. New life and growth is frequently associated with a 'devolution' of pastoral care. The traditional model of the local Church with its priest near to being 'Chaplain' to the membership is giving way to a more participative and dynamic model.

Empowering priesthood witnesses to the power of prayer. Many pastoral encounters involving priests or lay people with the needy fall short of leading people literally into prayer. Sometimes this omission reflects pastoral sensitivity. Other times there is a loss of both nerve and faith in the one who is pastorally active. Although it is not everyone's gift to talk naturally about God and to God, many more could discover this capacity. In the author's experience ending a pastoral encounter with a prayer brings out most fully the nature of what Christians call 'pastoral ministry'. If we see ourselves as instruments of God pointing people to God, how should it feel other than natural, whilst alongside people, to help them voice their expressed needs to God there and then?

THE MINISTRY OF BLESSING

Robin Greenwood speaks of the traditional priestly ministry of blessing: 'He has a particular role of blessing liturgically that is a mirror of his more general role of blessing. This is about encouraging (or inversely, discouraging) or as it were 'giving permission' (or not) to a step forward in mission or ministry…. It is so vital that the priest takes delight in drawing out the understanding, the skills, the commitment and the hope of every Church member. The ministry of blessing is about praising, encouraging, and expecting the growth in ministry of the whole of the body of the Church' (3).

The authority that is given to the priesthood to act in this way is directly linked to that of Christ himself, the Good Shepherd, in the ordination service: '(Priests) must set the Good Shepherd always before them… (they are to) grow up into (the Lord's) likeness and sanctify the lives of all with whom (they) have to do' (4). It is this security, sealed at ordination, which should help priests overcome their own by consciousness of their special anointing in the Holy Spirit. 'Such is the confidence that we have through Christ toward God. Not that we are competent of ourselves to claim anything as coming from us; our competence is from God, who has made us competent to be ministers of a new covenant, not of letter but of spirit; for the letter kills, but the Spirit gives life.' (2 Corinthians 3:4-6)

The recovery of such 'competence' among the ordained is a vital necessity, especially as it is linked in terms of the Gospel to their own need of grace and to the rejection of legalism. Where priests recognise the authority they have and use it to 'give authority' to others the Church's pastoral ministry develops. Failure to recognise this divine commission is behind much loss of energy and direction in the Church today. Misappropriation of the same authority to serve 'letter' before 'spirit' is equally damaging. Robert Warren describes 'the imperial - and in a double sense 'imposing' - approach to leadership which has 'the effect of making the laity second-class citizens and passive clients (or in today's terminology 'consumers') of the priestly professionals.'

Warren describes a confident 'missionary priesthood' in these words: 'They will need to be like conductors of an orchestra, drawing out the gifts of the many and finding how best to harmonise them. They will need to be emotionally secure, and neither threatened by gifted, visionary and able, lay-people, nor lacking the ability to stand over against the congregation, when necessary' (5).

In UK politics there is an ongoing debate about sovereignty in Britain vis-à-vis the EEC. Some see the nation losing power and vitality as European union advances. Others argue that loss of sovereignty can actually lead to the gain of power and vitality. It is this second argument that should appeal to the priest, who should be always ready to 'pool his "sovereignty"' as a gift from Christ to help empower lay ministries and to strengthen the body of Christ as a whole.

MAKING SPACE

A Churchwarden once paid an unusual compliment to his priest in conversation with the mission officer. 'What we like particularly about Fr. Peter is that he doesn't make us feel guilty when we occasionally miss meetings.' The man was managing director of a firm that took him all over Britain. Despite his most valiant efforts he could not always make it to Church meetings. No doubt Fr. Peter found it frustrating on the occasions Church officers were absent from important meetings. He refused however to show such frustration, always appearing to believe the best of absentees. Such a generous priest was helping to create a relaxed Church where grace and mercy triumphed over judgmental attitude.

Unfortunately the situation described is highly untypical of parish priests who are so often overworked themselves and can be very impatient with lay people who fail to volunteer effort or attendance. Diminishing membership puts heavy pressure upon smaller Churches and their priests in this realm.

One priest of my acquaintance has over his desk 'I am a human being, not a human doing'. Coping with stress is a major requirement for priests. Their failure to do so depresses their Church. Their ability to cope with pressure empowers and enthuses.

It was said of a late American Cardinal that 'when he sat down there was always more space'. To be serene and peaceful in the midst of the pressures of life is a pointer to the presence of an eternal perspective. It gives those nearby permission to be themselves, to enter the evident space and open themselves up to the priest and to God. It helps 'to equip the church for its mission of being fully human and participating in the humanising work of the kingdom of God' (Robert Warren).

An empowering priesthood is one modelled on both the energy and the availability of Jesus. It takes to heart the incident with the blind man in the Gospels. The Lord is at one time moving energetically to Jerusalem via Jericho. Yet in the tenth chapter of St. Mark's Gospel it is recorded that Jesus, though heading with the crowd to his passion, takes time to stop and to give his full attention to one blind man. 'What do you want me to do for you?'

How can priests make such space for people to do business with Jesus today? Although priests need prayer and discernment concerning their own availability, perhaps the first thing they have to recognise is that Jesus can make himself available through any Christian and not just the priest.

Making space for people to do business with God through the Church inevitably entails broadening the base of pastoral involvement. The widespread appointment of parish administrators is seen by parishes as a way of releasing the clergy from their desks. In some parishes with large home communion rounds authorised lay ministers operate three weeks out of four leaving the priest a monthly visit. In this way the priest can preside over a ministry whilst making space for ministries of listening and befriending beyond his own. The teaching ministry of priests is being similarly devolved in many parishes to house group leaders who are trained by the clergy.

PROMOTING FRIENDSHIP

Friendship is more and more recognised as being vital to healthy communities and Churches. Surveys of Church growth show how new members come into the life of the Church mostly through friendship with Church members. Some parish priests are becoming concerned to relax the demands of midweek activities with this in mind. Protecting the 'space' for the membership to be active in networks and personal relationships outside of the Church is good for them and for the growth of the Church.

The concept of 'friendship evangelism' is helpful to a point. True friendship has no agenda that overrides friendship for its own sake. At the same time, since friendship is based on honesty, to hide from friends how Christ helps our human and social flourishing would be dishonest. Ann Morisy writes of how the Church should be more confident about seizing occasions which crop up naturally in social engagements to help people 'do business with God'. Where there is space made for Church members to be themselves in any social network, the possibility of their quite naturally leading a prayer for a specific need that crops up cannot be excluded (6).

In a parish mission a Church member I visited as missioner had a friend she had been taking to the doctor every week. My visit had entered their conversation. As a result this lady welcomed the anointing of the sick at my hands and received a great sense of peace and blessing. Any healing that was given linked both to the sacramental rite with the priest and to the ongoing helpfulness of her Church friend.

There is an important principle here. Empowerment is the business of the Church because it has always the energy of Jesus Christ who sends us out in the power of his Spirit. An empowering priesthood recognises that ministry 'in the person of Christ' is one that they head up but one that is very often only 'headed up'. The 'body' of Christian ministry lies mostly elsewhere in the prayer and active service of all the baptised. It seemed especially important, during the rite of anointing of the sick lady, to invite her friend to join the priest in the laying on of hands to express such a 'concelebration' of Christ's healing.

Making space for lay ministries requires an investment of time by the clergy to help their development. It actually creates more pressure and potential stress upon priests when they commit themselves to a programme of lay training. In particular time spent with Church members equipping them is often subtracted from time spent by the priest in the wider community.

How do priests make space for themselves? How can they avoid being over-whelmed by the endless expectations upon them? How can they help the capturing of vision which will give the focus and direction needed in their parish?

Two gifts are necessary - *prayer* and *discernment* - and they are the subject of the next Chapter.

REFERENCES

1.   Eddie Gibbs *I Believe in Church Growth* 1981
2.   House of Bishops of the Church of England *A Time to Heal* 2000
3.   Robin Greenwood *Transforming Priesthood* 1994
4.   Ordination of Priests *The Alternative Service Book* 1980
5.   Robert Warren *Building Missionary Congregations* 1995
6.   Ann Morisy *Beyond the Good Samaritan* 1997

CHAPTER 6
WAITING FOR ORDERS

Walk with me - watch how I do it. Learn the unforced rhythms of grace. Matthew 11:29

The most common industrial injury at one time among the clergy was said to be a hernia caused by moving a heavy object unaided. This reveals a lot about the state of the priesthood - a degree of impatience and a reluctance to enlist lay ministry.

Sometimes priests feel they are 'pushing' alone. The boat of holy Church seems beached yet they get to pushing it out to sea. With the company of others the boat could be launched by human strength. It is best though to await the coming of the tide.

Empowering priesthood helps the Church await God's tide and timing as the best way of moving forwards together.

'The calling to ordained ministry with which I began had somehow been lost on the way, or overlaid by activity, or simply broken in the battle' writes Robert Warren. He was to see his priesthood instrumental in the empowering of St. Thomas, Sheffield which grew under his ministry from one hundred and fifty to over one thousand worshippers. He speaks of his ministry being transformed 'from achieving to receiving. I discovered that Christian service is all about God's plans, and God's grace to fulfil them, not about my plans to achieve things for God… I saw God as much more evidently the one calling the tune and pulling the strings. I saw him in a new way as the initiator of the Church's life and the writer of its agenda. I was moving from plans-to-serve-him to waiting-for-orders' (1).

THE UNFORCED RHYTHMS OF GRACE

One of the consequences of a more functional approach to the priesthood has been loss of emphasis on recollection as the clue to empowering. Sometimes the pressures on the ordained extend them so far outside and beyond their inner life that it can appear that 'no one is at home' within them.

How many priests, when apparently listening, have most of their deep attention in the next task? We have so many 'plans-to-serve-him' we have no space for his empowering of ministry in the present moment. Into this situation, again and again, we need to hear the words of Jesus.

'Are you tired? Burned out in religion? Come to me get away with me and you will recover your life. I'll show you how to take a real rest. Walk with me - watch how I do it. Learn the unforced rhythms of grace. I won't lay anything heavy or ill-fitting you. Keep company with me and you'll learn to live freely and lightly' (Matthew 11: 28-30 from The Message (2)).

Empowerment comes to priests and Churches as they discover the 'unforced rhythms of grace'. There is no forcing of the will of God for individuals or community.

Only by patient, prayerful discernment can real advances occur, as there is a purification and alignment of human intention with divine providence. 'All that we do is nothing worth unless God blesses the deed' is hard counsel in its challenging of self-determination by individuals or Churches.

Monsignor Ronald Knox in his book 'The Priestly Life' has a clever definition of idleness. 'Idleness is not doing nothing; it means giving priority, always, to the things which interest and leaving our other duties to queue up.' (3) In other words the clue to priestly zeal is developing such an interest in the things of God that our priorities are sifted accordingly.

We reach the 'unforced rhythms of grace' only by deepening our attention upon the Lord himself, notably by setting apart a generous period of prayer day by day. In this way something of God's eternal perspective is obtained for daily living, sifting the important matters for our attention from the merely urgent matters. Ironically it is this forced discipline of daily prayer that seems essential to 'unforced' living. Those who adopt such a discipline will readily confirm the consequences of dropping their prayer from time to time. The people to be seen, the writing to be done and the services to be conducted weigh heavily and have no harmony about them. Priests need to give wholehearted attention to such a variety of people, issues and situations that they need a special gift of attention. Where can grace to sustain such attention be obtained if it is not sought in prayer?

THE GIFT OF DISCERNMENT

'Never before have human beings had as much spare time as today, and never yet have they had as little time... Although the world offers us unlimited possibilities, our own lifespans are short. Hence many people panic because they think they might miss something, and thus accelerate the tempo of their lives... A person who lives ever faster so as not to miss anything always lives superficially and misses the deeper experiences of life. Everything is possible in that person's world but only very little is real.' (4)

Without discernment human beings get overstretched by the pressures of life. There can hardly be empowerment in a life that has no discerned path since all energy is rapidly dispersed. A similar dynamic applies to the Christian community as a whole. Some Churches have a rich diversity of activity which seems to lead them nowhere in particular. In such situations there is a need to discern priorities and to capture unifying and directing vision from the Lord.

'Test everything; hold fast to what is good; abstain from every form of evil.' (1 Thessalonians 5: 21-22) St. Paul's counsel on discernment calls for a testing through God-given reason and God-given faith. Reason and faith - both matter. There are two undergirding theological truths in the matter of discernment, those of creation and redemption. In 'waiting for orders' - for our life or for our Church - practical down-to-earth reason matters, alongside the spiritual gift of discernment. For example stress problems may be solved by setting one's alarm or going to bed early as much as by prayer for inner healing. What matters is to discern from among the many demands put upon us what we are to 'hold fast to', which is God's will at that time, and let go of the rest. One sign of correct discernment is the adoption of a more outward-looking attitude which reflects fresh capturing of the perspective and energy of Jesus Christ.

An empowering priesthood ministers in such a way as to help individual Church members discern and loosen unhealthy attachments. The pressures of modern living make for a profound loss of energy through regret and anxiety. With so much opportunity people lose inner energy through their regrets about lost opportunity. They also lose energy to anxiety about so many fearful possibilities. Where people discern their attachment to such fears they are in a position to break the bonds and claim new freedom and energy in Christ.

Empowering priesthood recognises that lack of empowerment in the Church very often comes back to forms of over-attachment that need gentle but firm challenge in individuals and congregations. Sometimes the answer to fresh empowerment is right under our noses if only we can discern it.

LIFTING THE STONES

When God sent a vision to Bernadette in 1854 it was to have consequences for the whole world. Millions go on pilgrimage to Lourdes and bathe to this day in the healing waters. The stream of water was actually released by directions given to St. Bernadette in one of her visions of the Blessed Virgin Mary. She was told to dig in the ground and remove a heap of earth and stones. As she dug down the stream began, and it has never stopped flowing since.

There is a parable here of spiritual discernment and empowerment. Like Bernadette we need guidance to lift the stones that stem the flow of life-giving streams both within us and also within the life of the Church as a whole. Sometimes the erosion of our faith has placed a stone over the fountain. Other times broken relationships in need of repair are causing spiritual life to dry up inside us or inside the Christian community. It is then that a seeking of vision from God can have enormous impact as he shows us just where to dig to release his life.

'On the last day of the festival, the great day, while Jesus was standing there, he cried out, "Let anyone who is thirsty come to me, and let the one who believes in me drink. As the scripture has said, 'Out of the believer's heart shall flow rivers of living water.' Now he said this about the Spirit, which believers in him were going to receive.' (John 7: 37-9a)

One of the things that weigh down upon spiritual vitality is tidy-mindedness. Many priests like things too neat. The Holy Spirit is not always tidy-minded and is certainly not small-minded! Empowering priesthood is priesthood that can recognise and ridicule its own small-mindedness and help others to do the same, whilst capturing the larger vision of what the Spirit is doing and wants to do in a community.

VISION AND VITALITY

It is the quality of attentiveness to God and to one another that helps priest and people discern what is needed in the parish. Only through such discernment can parish life be given suitable direction. As previously mentioned in Chapter 4 there is always creative tension between the 'cyclical' and 'directional' aspects in the life of the Church. Whilst the 'cyclical' aspects of Church life, her repeated feasts and social events, remain foundational, they are to be balanced by a 'directional' element. The pilgrim people of God are called to seek and follow the Lord's leading aided at times by their prophets.

Ann Morisy describes how a nun's prayer for the homeless so burdened her she began to investigate ways they might be served in her town and ended up recruiting a team to serve them. 'A prayer burden may ultimately lead to action, as it did for Sister Teresa, but at a minimum it commits us to a struggle which is wider than self-concern.' The vision which started in one woman's prayer and imagination came to bear fruit in a vital ministry of service and outreach (5).

Empowering priesthood recognises that 'without vision, the people perish' (Proverbs 29:18). Waiting together for orders from on high finds its reward in the revelation of way forwards that excite motivation within the Christian community.

In a diocese the diversity of parishes makes the catching and ownership of a central vision a perilous business. One of the difficulties is building sufficient involvement and trust among priests and among parishes to establish a genuine communality. Parish priests share their ministry with the bishop as 'apostle' in the diocese. When there is a partnership 'apostolic' in both an institutional and missionary sense a powerful spiritual prioritisation emerges within the Christian community.

In the years before the consecration of Coventry Cathedral in 1963 Bishop Cuthbert Bardsley brought to his diocese the vision of a consecrated people. Such was the ownership of the vision that some of the Clergy Chapters began to meet weekly to pray. It was a period in which a high degree of trust and openness to one another and to God emerged among priests and people in Coventry Diocese. Even to this day people recall the extraordinary envisioning of those days and there are many that can trace the kindling of their vocation back to the apostolic vitality of that diocesan initiative. (6)

Empowering priesthood is always by its nature in partnership with the episcopate. Where this partnership captures 'the abiding energy of Jesus Christ' there is a particularly convincing apostolic mandate. 'As the Father has sent me, even so I send you' (John 20:21).

REFERENCES

1.   Robert Warren *On the Anvil* 1990
2.   Eugene Peterson *The Message* 1993
3.   Ronald Knox *The Priestly Life* 1958
4.   Jurgen Moltmann *St. Paul's Cathedral Lecture on Preparing for the Third Christian Millennium* 1998
5.   Ann Morisy *Beyond the Good Samaritan* 1997
6.   Stephen Verney *Fire in Coventry* 1964

CHAPTER 7
SEEKING TRANSFORMATION

Empowering priesthood catalyses ministries that invite transformation and not just the serving of need

In 1988 the Lambeth Conference of Anglican Bishops challenged their dioceses to seek 'a shift to a dynamic missionary emphasis, going beyond care and nurture to proclamation and service' (1). This became a foundational statement for the Decade of Evangelism now completed.

Among the more radical contributions to thinking in the Church of England during the Decade stands an occasional paper of the Board of Mission, 'Building Missionary Congregations' (2). Robert Warren calls there for a 'reshaping of the Church' and a 'restoring purpose' to its nature. Warren's own experience of Church growth gave him confidence to present a trenchant challenge to the status quo. His book contains much wisdom about recovering vision in the local Church.

Where it most falls short is in its lack of regard for the ordained ministry as servants of the recovery of 'a dynamic missionary emphasis'. In particular the definition of the Church in terms of mission neglects consideration of her first priority. Worship is considered mainly as servant of spirituality for mission rather than for what it is in itself - the giving of glory to God. The radical nature of this book is made clear in its preface by the Chairman of the Board of Mission who stresses that both 'revolutionists' and 'evolutionists' must have their say about future directions.

If 'evolutionists' are to speak out in any sphere that complements the thinking of 'Building Missionary Congregations' it should be concerning the gift of the priesthood as servant of empowering. 'You cannot sustain a missionary congregation', writes John Finney. 'It is like a ring doughnut, there is nothing at the centre.' Engaging with this observation Warren admits that 'a missionary congregation is one which sees its calling as both to be and to tell the good news. It is a community whose life consists in the celebration and enjoyment of the liberating wholeness of Jesus Christ'. Yet it is precisely the role of priests to guarantee through their office this complementarity of worship and mission and the very centring of both in the energy of Jesus Christ. 'Forget the priesthood and the Church becomes an institution for man's conversion instead of a spiritual temple for God's worship' (Box).

If the call for a 'dynamic missionary emphasis' is to gain new momentum it will be as the Church renews her confidence in the ministerial priesthood as one of his gifts of empowerment.

EFFECTIVE SIGNS

In developing the theme of an empowering priesthood, attention has been given extensively to the centrality of Jesus and how priests act for him in a particular way.

It is the particular function of priests to call down the Holy Spirit and 'make present to his people the work of Jesus Christ' (3). This can and should make an enormous difference to people's lives.

As traditionally understood, sacraments are effective signs, rites that change things for people in both senses of that phrase. As the risen Christ used signs to make himself known after his resurrection, so the same Lord Jesus, since Pentecost, is seen to be manifested, and particularly through the sacramental ministries of those called to represent him in the priesthood.

Sacraments are no empty rituals - or at least that is meant to be the Christian conviction. By the power of the Holy Spirit Christ renews his presence and that presence brings about transformation. Sadly, Christians have divided over the priority of the subjective and objective aspects of this manifestation. There have been times when the sacraments have appeared empty of Christ through their unworthy and mechanical celebration so that people sought a vital relationship with Christ elsewhere in ministries of prayer and of the word of God.

Empowering priesthood is a priesthood that brings together what history has sundered so that Christ is recognised in both word and sacrament. Where Christ is preached, the Eucharist becomes more fully his sacrifice as people more consciously offer themselves in union with him to the Father. Where Christ is encountered at a deep level in the sacraments, a hunger for the scriptures is born.

On the Emmaus Road, the disciples who encountered the risen Christ in 'the breaking of bread' also recalled how their hearts burned as the same Christ 'was opening the scriptures to us' (Luke 24:13-25). In the same way the vitality of Christ is encountered day by day by Christians through scripture and sacrament.

CHANGED LIVES

'We must not suppose that even if we succeeded in making everyone nice we should have saved their souls...mere improvement is not redemption... ' warned C.S.Lewis. 'God became man to turn creatures into sons: not simply to produce better men of the old kind but to produce a new kind of man. It is not like teaching a horse to jump better and better but like turning a horse into a winged creature.' (4).

An empowering priesthood sees itself as instrumental to this business of transforming rather than improving people. Priestly ministry helps effect encounters of disciples with their Lord and their consequent transformation.

'All of us, with unveiled faces, seeing the glory of the Lord as though reflected in a mirror, are being transformed into the same image from one degree of glory to another; for this comes from the Lord, the Spirit' (2 Corinthians 3:18).

How can priests be more effective instruments serving such transformation?

The most precious resource in evangelism are changed lives, people who can speak of the difference Jesus has made to them. Sometimes the transformations people can speak of are astounding. Other times they give testimony to a more gentle, gradual transformation. Every Church should have evidence of how Christ is growing more real to people. One of the tasks of the priesthood is to help the Christian community grow confident enough to voice their experience in all its diversity.

Karl Rahner once made this prophecy, which must be heeded, today in the Church: 'The religious person of the future will either be one who has experienced something or he will no longer exist' (5).

One of the tasks of the sacred ministry is to give ear to and to affirm and encourage the experience of the sacred that is so vital to the health and growth of the Church. It is a task that requires humility in a priest. Sacred ministers are not set apart to be necessarily holier than the next Christian but to give space to the priority of spiritual transformation. It is their own sense of inadequacy in this realm that is in principle their best resource. Too often a lack of readiness to thank God for other people's blessings stalls this sort of prioritising. There is also a fear of public statements with weak theology about them.

The great Archbishop Temple spoke powerfully to such reservations: 'It does very little harm if an eager layman talks heresy, provided he shows and imparts a love for the Lord Jesus. It does great harm if a priest talks orthodoxy so as to make men think the Gospel is dull or irrelevant' (6).

GOING OUT ON A LIMB

In the training of priests there is an inevitable stress upon systematic, balanced theology. There is a reluctance to economise, to throw out a provocative line to challenge. Evangelistic preaching is always a shade unbalanced, going out on a limb deliberately to provoke a personal response to Christ. It requires courage and imagination to address people's needs with urgency, requiring a decision for the Lord. Concern for balance has its place in the overall teaching and preaching scheme but it has to give way at times to words that shock and challenge by their immediacy and directness.

Raniero Cantalamessa gives a similar warning: 'The *fides quae* (the things to be believed - catechesis) have carried the day against the *fides qua* (the act of faith - evangelisation). The miracle of coming to faith has less stress today than the completeness and orthodoxy of the content of faith itself' (7).

Recovering an emphasis on 'the miracle of coming to faith' is a grace to be sought out within the overall catechetical ministry. The success of the Alpha Course lies in its simple summary of Christian Faith providing enough of a basis to provoke personal commitment to Christ and empowering by the Holy Spirit (8). Many have criticised it for its economy and oversimplification. Those whose lives have been transformed by attending Alpha tell a different story. They say they have found enough 'lines' thrown out at them over the fifteen sessions to facilitate a grasping of

Christian Faith. Naturally they will move on from Alpha and with receptivity to fuller catechesis, to 'the whole counsel of God' (Acts 20:27 RSV).

SEEKING COMMITMENT

An empowering priesthood is one that sees Christian formation going beyond the intellectual to the volitional, the consecration of the will to God, which is the recipe for transformation. This is nothing new. Preparation for the sacraments, especially Confirmation, has always emphasised growth in relationship to Christ as foundational. The involvement of mature Christians in this process guarantees a sharing of experience that goes beyond knowledge of the things of God towards the knowledge of God himself. As in the Alpha Course, effective Christian teaching makes space for people to raise questions central to their lives. In this way, aided by the Christian community, they are able to do personal business with God.

Preparation for infant baptism seems most effective when it both makes space and allowance for the parents, with all the demands young children make upon them, whilst giving them the clear invitation to commit themselves to Christ on behalf of their children. The balance of welcome, challenge and empowerment there is in Jesus needs to be perceived in his priestly body. Where people respond to Jesus through the Church and commit themselves they become vital resource people for subsequent baptism preparation, real catalysts of spiritual transformation.

Long term Church members who restrict their involvement to Sunday worship can fail to find opportunity to connect their perceived needs with the resources of the Faith. The late American evangelist, John Wimber described his experience of the Church in England in a telling sentence: 'When I worship in English churches I detect in the congregations a remarkably high level of personal need, matched by a correspondingly low level of expectation'.

EXPECTING TRANSFORMATION

In many inner city Churches almost all energy is taken up from the clergy and lay ministers in serving their evidently needy members. There is much loving care but, as Wimber expresses it, 'low level of expectation' of Jesus making a difference. Sometimes this situation indicates a pastoral mode of the Church negligent of the prophetic and empowering emphases.

In some Churches the members have had no experience of the miracle of people making a transition from agnosticism to faith although such miracles continue day by day. Rahner by contrast writes boldly of the importance of such conversions: 'The possibility of winning new Christians from a milieu which has become unchristian is the sole living and convincing evidence that, even today, Christianity still has a real chance for the future...it means more to win one new Christian from what we may call neo-paganism, than to keep ten 'old Christians" (9).

Where a congregation is privileged to encounter such vivid transformations there is a ripple effect renewing faith expectancy. 'It is for this reason that I covet for every Christian, whether he be one of the clergy or of the laity, that from time to time he may have the privilege of being at hand when God breaks into someone's soul. It freshens, deepens and beautifies with an all-pervading warmth the whole of our ministry.' (10)

Empowering priesthood catalyses ministries that invite transformation and not just the serving of need. Jesus meets us at our point of need to lead us on into transformation. There are many instances in the Gospels of lives touched at a specific point of need that are subsequently transformed into wholehearted commitment. The loss of expectation that Christianity can follow the same course today needs to be challenged.

At the same time priests have the balancing task of challenging oversimple views of transformation. On occasion people have been led to overplay the role of spiritual experience to the detriment of the virtues of obedience and perseverance.

There is a cautionary story of St. Seraphim of Sarov being asked why it is that some people seem to get the Holy Spirit more than others. 'Just determination' was his answer.

Though virtues like determination cannot earn salvation, they dispose people towards Christ in an ongoing way. It appears that the Lord is more interested in the firmness of our desire for him than in anything else about us. The faithfulness and determination of priests does much to inspire these essential qualities in the membership of their Churches.

CONSECRATING STRENGTH

Empowerment involves the release of potential energy in the Church. It is a locating and releasing of gifts and strengths. The consecration of human strength to God's praise and service is at the heart of evangelisation.

Dietrich Bonhoeffer had a particular emphasis in his writings upon the consecration of strength. He once wrote, for example, that Napoleon's sin lay probably more in his misuse of strength than in his sexual misdemeanours. As Bonhoeffer's own martyrdom by the Nazi's itself witnesses, the worst damage done to the world is done through the misuse of strength rather than through human frailty.

Some priests are given a vital charism. They accomplish the consecration of the strong. Sometimes at a word or by a glance, people find themselves caught into service with a new direction for their lives. It is said of St. Ignatius Loyola that as a young man he visited a good number of priests to discuss the existence of God. One day he met his match in a priest who would not enter discussion but rather insisted that he made his Confession. This priest apparently provided an important stage in the harnessing of Ignatius' great energies for the Church.

Dom Helder Camera died in 1999 having spent his life in the service of the Brazilian poor. He abandoned his bishop's palace to live among the poor, took his meals at the taxi-drivers stall across the road and hitched lifts instead of riding in his official car. He became a great pioneer of the social gospel. Yet when he tells the tale of his life it is more the mystical than the practical that takes precedence. He said the biggest change in his life came not from the poor but from an encounter with a Cardinal he served in organising the big Eucharistic Congress of 1955 in Rio de Janeiro. Cardinal Gerlier of France, moved by what he saw of Rio's shanty towns, put it to Dom Helder that he would better put his organising talents to the service of the poor. Camera writes: 'And so the grace of the Lord came to me through the presence of Cardinal Gerlier. Not just through the words he spoke: behind his words was the presence of a whole life, a whole conviction. And I was moved by the grace of the Lord. I was thrown to the ground like Saul on the road to Damascus.' Through this powerful encounter with a great priest Camera's gifts became more fully consecrated to the service of God's kingdom. (11)

Such encounters with holy people are at the heart of all effective evangelisation. 'When a person awakens to the awareness of God around them, the light of this belonging suffuses their presence and radiates outwards from them. This is natural, wholesome and authentic. In the end the most effective and trustable witness is the integrity of individual presence.' (12)

REFERENCES

1. Lambeth Conference *Recommendation 44* 1988
2. Robert Warren *Building Missionary Congregations* 1995
3. General Synod Report *Priesthood of the Ordained Ministry* 1986
4. C.S.Lewis *Mere Christianity* 1952
5. Quoted in G. Guiver et al *The Fire and the Clay* 1993
6. Archbishop William Temple in *Towards the Conversion of England* 1945
7. Raniero Cantalamessa *The Holy Spirit in the Life of Jesus* 1994
8. Holy Trinity, Brompton *The Alpha Course* 1993
9. Karl Rahner *The Shape of the Church to Come* 1972
10. Bryan Green *The Practice of Evangelism* 1951
11. Jose de Brouker *Dom Helder Camera: the conversions of a bishop* 1979
12. John O'Donohue *Article in The Way, Vol. 34, No. 4* 1994

CHAPTER 8
LOOKING TO JESUS

Look, Father, look on His anointed face, and only look on us as found in Him. W. Bright

Churches Together in England expressed the challenge of the Third Christian Millennium as one inviting the Churches 'to forge a link in people's minds between the year 2000, the name of Jesus Christ, and the possibility of personal meaning and public hope' (1).

In many ways the recovery of an empowering priesthood is linked to the recovering of the centrality of Jesus in the Church today. It is the work of the Holy Spirit to draw the Christian community again and again to proclaim 'Jesus is Lord' (1 Corinthians 12:3). The recovery of the lordship of Jesus is at the heart of the experience of revival in the Church all through her history. Renewal of vision is a challenging of attitudes that 'make God smaller than the God who has revealed himself to us in Jesus' (2).

Michael Ramsey speaks of the inspiration to be drawn by priests from dwelling on the person of Jesus who blends 'authority and self-effacement, severity and tenderness, loneliness and involvement in humanity, ceaseless energy and rest and calm in the midst of it'. 'Teach them not only the Real Presence in the Eucharist but about Christ whose presence it is...Your own ministration will need again and again to be made alive by your own realisation of Christ'. 'When you promise to minister the doctrine of Christ', he says in an ordination address, 'it will mean showing the people Christ himself'.

True empowerment relies on the power of Christ. 'who has became a priest, not through a legal requirement concerning physical descent but through the power of an indestructible life' (Hebrews 7:16).

'All Christian ministry finds its source, its model and its authority in the ministry of Jesus', writes Gordon Kuhrt, who goes on to identify five aspects of the ministry of Jesus that should challenge Christian ministry today. There is a modelling of Jesus who is 'sent by God; witness to God's Kingdom by preaching, teaching and signs; ministering to human need through care and healing; servant-like in attitude and filled by God's Spirit' (3).

MAKING CHRIST'S PRIESTHOOD PRESENT

Kuhrt affirms that 'in spite of all the frailties and failures of the Church's life (Jesus) is its *source* - for he calls his people to ministry; its *model* for he is the example of ministry; and its *authority* - for he commissions and empowers through his Spirit. There is discontinuity because of the ultra uniqueness of Christ, but we must, nevertheless, keep looking to Jesus, the great Shepherd of the sheep (Hebrews 12:2, 13:20).

He is himself critical of the idea of a ministerial priesthood representing Jesus out of deference to the Reformed tradition within the Church of England. At the same time he well represents the traditional view through extensive quotation from the Report 'Priesthood of the Ordained Ministry' which affirms the Christocentric understanding of Ordination.

'(Ordained) ministry is not simply delegated by or derived from the community. It is argued that theirs is a distinctively different form of priestly ministry in that (to quote the Report) it 'is an appointed means through which Christ makes his priesthood present and effective to his people...Their (episcopal and presbyteral) ministry may be called priestly in that it is their vocation to help the whole people to realise their priestly character... It is in the particular relationship of the Eucharist and the ministry of reconciliation to the sacrifice of Christ that the priestly character of the ordained ministry is most evident. This ministry is priestly because through it God makes present to his people the work of Jesus Christ, the mediator who brings humanity to God' (3, 4)

MATTERS OF PRINCIPLE

Sadly the empowering of the priesthood within Anglicanism at least is hampered by the Reformation divisions. As Kuhrt notes, for many 'the concept of a ministerial sacrificial priesthood is unscriptural.' As an Anglican writer seeking to do justice to both Catholic and Reformed traditions he seeks no 'careless compromise, but rather a principled agenda to take what is right and best of those traditions and weave them together. That is not an easy task… we do nobody any favours either by judging the issues or by unnecessarily polarising them.'

If clarity about the nature of the ministerial priesthood has no consensus as yet in Anglicanism hope for convergence must lie somehow in 'looking to Jesus' (Hebrews 12:2) with the whole Church to catch afresh both vision and empowerment.

The polemical statement 'no man between myself and God' must be honoured in as much as it seeks to look to Jesus. Those who see Christ as 'coming between our souls and God' and hold to his representation by earthly priests must be aware of the real danger of idolatry. It was said of Fr. Raymond Raynes of the Community of the Resurrection that he had the gift of engaging people through his representative priesthood so as to pass them straight on to the Jesus he represented. His transparency to Christ was exceptional. Most priests are less adequate vehicles of Christ.

'For there is one God; there is also one mediator between God and humankind, Christ Jesus, himself human.' (1 Timothy 2:5) Is the unique mediation of Christ undermined by the ministry of intercession and of priesthood? If all prayer and sacramental ministry is perceived as 'through him, with him and in him' there is in principle no subtraction from the mediation of Christ. His prayer and sacrifice rise up from his body, which has imparted to it all 'the benefits of his passion'.

Someone who sees a prayer answered 'in the name of Jesus' could not arrogate to themselves the cause of such a supernatural intervention. No more can the Church's liturgical prayer, which brings about the sacramental presence of her Lord, be so arrogated to her apart from Christ. 'For man hath no oblation more worthy nor any satisfaction greater for putting away of sins, than to offer himself to God purely and wholly, *together with the oblation of the Body of Christ* in the Mass and in receiving the communion' (5).

ACCEPTED IN THE BELOVED SON

Both Catholic and Reformed traditions 'look to Jesus' in the sense of deeply appreciating that access to God and intimacy with him is fully established in him alone. They also hold that it is 'the abiding energy of Jesus Christ' that empowers the Church's mission.

At its best the emphasis on the Eucharist as sacrifice is faithful to the unique mediation of Christ given to allow the consecration and empowering of Christians as they unite their lives to his.

> 'Look, Father, look on His anointed face, and only look on us as found in Him;
> Look not on our misusings of Thy grace, our prayer so languid, and our faith so dim:
> For lo! Between our sins and their reward we set the passion of Thy Son our Lord' (W. Bright, Hymns Ancient and Modern).

Before his ascension Jesus promised the disciples 'I am ascending to my Father and your Father, to my God and your God' (John 20:17b). By looking to Jesus they will be drawn into the intimacy of the Son for the Father and the Father for the Son at the heart of the redemption. The ascended Christ is also the one who will empower for mission by his Spirit (Acts 1:8, Ephesians 4:8-12).

Empowering priesthood helps effect the continuation of Christ's ministry, which draws people to intimacy with the Father and reaches out from the Father into the world. In a phrase of Austin Farrer, priests are 'walking sacraments'. They exist to point with Christ to his twofold intention of 'the glory of God and the salvation of the world'.

The choice of sinful human beings to be his representatives is ultimately *his* choice. Some may argue whether an individual can act 'alter Christus', as an 'other Christ', but when the argument against is pressed it ultimately conflicts with the dignity given to every Christian. 'Whoever welcomes you welcomes me' (Matthew 10:40a). All Christians are inadequate representatives of their Lord. The fact that some are called as reminders to the whole body of the centrality of Christ is servant and not rival of that essential centrality.

It is reasonable to see empowerment in the Church as achievable through a dispersal of authority from priest to congregation. Yet in this 'reasonable' process it is very easy to lose the essential Christocentric focus and impetus, to which the apostolic ministry bears witness. 'All authority in heaven and on earth has been given to me' (Matthew 28:18). 'As the Father has sent me, so I send you' (John 20:21).

Empowering priesthood is priesthood pointing people to Jesus and to the intimacy he brings with God. The priest's traditional role in eucharistic worship is to be a 'walking sacrament' of Jesus. His role, as was said of Fr. Raynes, is to draw people through his office as priest to Jesus Christ himself.

Unfortunately division over the nature of the Eucharist and the priesthood has led to something of a downplaying of the role of Christ with new emphasis upon the Trinity as a whole in contemporary reflections in these realms. Although Christian worship is addressed to the Trinity, the miracle of access to the Father is always the work of Jesus Christ in the power of the Holy Spirit. Ministerial priesthood serves to guarantee this centrality of Christ which establishes 'a spiritual temple for God's worship' (Box.).

WE WISH TO SEE JESUS

'By ordination, a Christian becomes a sign of the ministry of Jesus Christ in his Church.' (Max Thurian) If this is so, the question is one of renewing the sign and all that would obscure it. 'We wish to see Jesus' (John 12:21).

In his influential writings Hans Von Balthasar presents precisely such a call, affirmative of the priest as sign of Christ, yet insistent on radical imitation of the Lord. Dermot Power interprets Balthasar's writing on the priesthood as inviting 'an utter dependence on faith that allows the priest to live out of a sense of dependence on the power and presence of Christ, and not something less'. This 'something less' includes for Balthasar 'dependence on intra-ecclesial status, power and an over-reliance on ministerial skills and professional competence… it is the criterion of where the ultimate security of the priesthood lies that is the crucial test of its authenticity. To be truly authentic, the priesthood must make itself defenceless to the nakedness of faith and to the absolute demand of the Gospel' (6).

Looking to Jesus in this way takes the ordained ministry right back to its New Testament rooting it in the imitation and bearing of Christ. 'For whenever I am weak, then I am strong' (2 Corinthians 12:10), words that resonate with the earlier teaching of St Paul in that letter. Here it is made clear that because the apostle's commission or office is of God, it is to be carried in all humility. 'We have this treasure in clay jars' (4:7) is teaching that can apply to any Christian but holds special force for those in the apostolic ministry.

An empowering priesthood helps people '(look) to Jesus, the pioneer and perfecter of our faith' (Hebrews 12:2) to gain energy from him. It is a ministry of prayer, word and sacrament, teaching and pastoral care that recalls the promise of the Lord himself. 'I, when I am lifted up from the earth, will draw all people to myself' (John 12:32).

'I sometimes put this question to myself', wrote Ramsey. 'Looking back to all the sermons I have preached in the past, say six months, what have they told the people about Christ or done to make Christ visible to them? Do they know more about Christ at the end of them?' (2).

When lay people complained that they could not see the consecrated bread at Mass in the Middle Ages, they made the following entreaty: 'Heave it higher, Sir Priest'. This is said to be the origin of the traditional elevation of the host and chalice still practised in the Church at the Eucharist. The practice has been debated, particularly with respect to the almost magical approach to the sacramental consecration it can cultivate. The instinct of the medieval laity however may not have been so far from that of St Philip's Greek companions who 'wished to see Jesus' (John 12:21).

THE GOSPEL IN FOUR WORDS

Empowering priesthood makes the most of that empowering promise, 'this is my body', since it resonates with the very centre of Christian Faith in the self-giving of Jesus. 'At the heart of our lives is the celebration of that moment of utter vulnerability and generosity, when Jesus took bread and broke it and gave it to his disciples saying 'Take and eat, this is my body, given to you.' At the centre of the gospel is a moment of pure gift. This is where the *caritas* which is the life of God becomes most tangible. It is a generosity that our society finds hard to grasp, for our society is a market in which everything is bought and sold. What sense can it make of the God who shouts out 'Come to me all who are thirsty and I will give you food without price' (7).

The priest who blesses bread and wine in the name of the Lord continually draws the Church back to this mystery of God's self-giving in Jesus Christ. 'This is my body'. Here is the Gospel in four words, in presence and in power. Here is the faithfulness of God disclosed 'unto death'. Christians are here recalled to the central truth of the Faith, the gift of Jesus Christ himself. It is a generosity that plants itself in all who see and welcome Jesus continuously present to his people particularly through the Eucharist.

The honouring of the sacramental presence of Jesus has its place, but that honouring should extend to the other ways in which he is made present through prayer, scripture and through the gathering of the congregation. 'For where two or three are gathered in my name, I am there among them.' (Matthew 18:20) The late Ian Petit, a Benedictine Monk, talked of his own experience of lifting up the host at Mass facing the people. Originally taught to keep his eyes upon the consecrated bread, he explained how his own devotion came to have eyes for both the host and the people on the other side of it. For both it was true to say 'this is my body'.

This study of the priesthood began with the call for renewed 'horizons and visions of its meaning and truth'. It concludes by underlining the words of Jesus which interpret the ultimate horizon, words put on the lips of priests in particular. It is the self-giving of Jesus that both establishes and authenticates an empowering priesthood. By calling the Church back day by day to this mystery the ordained become a renewal gift of the ascended Christ. Where their own lives reflect this 'downward mobility of God' (Henri Nouwen), their priesthood is one that uplifts the Church.

'Therefore, since we are surrounded by so great a cloud of witnesses, let us also lay aside every weight and the sin that clings so closely, and let us run with perseverance the race that is set before us, looking to Jesus...' (Hebrews 12:1-2a).

REFERENCES

1.   Churches Together in England *A Chance to Start Again* 1996
2.   Michael Ramsey *The Christian Priest Today* 1972
3.   Gordon Kuhrt *An Introduction to Christian Ministry* 2000
4.   General Synod Report 694 *Priesthood of the Ordained Ministry* 1986
5.   Thomas a Kempis (1380-1471) *The Imitation of Christ*
6.   Dermot Power *A Spiritual Theology of the Priesthood* 1998
7.   Timothy Radcliffe *Sing a New Song* 1999

A PRAYER FOR PRIESTS

Lord Jesus,
you have chosen your priests from among us
and sent them out to proclaim your word
and to act in your name.
For so great a gift to your Church,
we give you praise and thanksgiving.
We ask you to fill them
with the fire of your love,
that their ministry may reveal
your presence in the Church.
Since they are earthen vessels,
we pray that your power
shine out through their weakness.
In their afflictions let them never be crushed;
in their doubts never despair;
in temptation never be destroyed;
in persecution never abandoned.
Inspire them through prayer to live each day
the mystery of your dying and rising.
In times of weakness send them your Spirit,
and help them to praise your heavenly Father
and pray for poor sinners.
By the same Holy Spirit
put your words on their lips
and your love in their hearts,
to bring good news to the poor
and healing to the brokenhearted.

www.intercessionforpriests.org